THROUGH THE BACK DOOR

MEMOIRS OF A SHARECROPPER'S DAUGHTER WHO LEARNED TO READ AS A GREAT-GRANDMOTHER

by

JANET DRISKELL TURNER

Authors Choice Press

New York   Lincoln   Shanghai

Through the Back Door
Memoirs of a Sharecropper's Daughter
Who Learned to Read as a Great-Grandmother

All Rights Reserved © 2001, 2004 by Janet Driskell Turner

No part of this book may be reproduced or transmitted in any form or by any means, graphic, electronic, or mechanical, including photocopying, recording, taping, or by any information storage or retrieval system, without the written permission of the publisher.

Authors Choice Press
an imprint of iUniverse, Inc.

For information address:
iUniverse, Inc.
2021 Pine Lake Road, Suite 100
Lincoln, NE 68512
www.iuniverse.com

Originally published by Creativa Press

ISBN: 0-595-32450-9

Printed in the United States of America

In Memory of

Mom, Dad, Big Mama,
and my husband, Mack
You made life fun.
I miss your laugh.

To my sisters and brothers and their families.
Lord bless each and every one.

I love you all.

For information about BoulderReads!
visit: **www.boulderreads.org**

Table of Contents

Acknowledgements vi
Foreword vii
Introduction ix
When I Was Born 1
Our Lives Are a Gift of God: Not by Years, But One Day at a Time . . . 3
Life in the South 6
My Worst Nightmare 12
The Good Old Days 13
Big Mama 18
In Those Days, You Could Not Afford to Get Sick 20
Where Babies Come From 21
Struggling to Survive 22
Namesake 24
Funerals 26
The Bell 27
Determined 28
Going to School 29
Christmas at School 31
Church 32
The Gathering 36
Getting into Trouble 40
I Made a Promise to Daddy 42
Standing Up to People 44
No Respect for Blacks 45
White Man's Rules 46
Doing the Right Thing 48
Losing Dad and Mom 55
Going Back, Being Free 56
The Voice 60
My Husband, Mack 61
My Father-in law, General Lee 64
Having a Job and Saving Money 66
Learning How to Live without Mack 69
Learning to Read 72
Parkinson's 79
Perfect Day with My Tutor 81
Time Capsule 83

Acknowledgements

I want to thank all the people who touched my life along the way, especially the special ladies that put up with me: Diana Sherry, Director of the Boulder Public Library's BoulderReads!; JoAnn Brothers, Helen Schweizer, Ruth Rettich and Diane Quint, my tutors in BoulderReads!; my friend and neighbor, Paula Henderson; and my friend and editor, Loretta Goodenbour. These ladies were always ready to help me in any way they could.

My thanks to Angela Beloian for illustrating the cover and Greg Ravenwood for helping with the layout. I also want to thank Laurie Watkins of BoulderReads! for always helping and always encouraging me. I want to thank Terri Malucci of creativa press for helping with publication, and Linda Andrews for reviewing the book. And I especially want to thank the Boulder Public Library Foundation which gave us a grant that helped cover the printing.

The Carrolls* and Mrs. Barton* made me a part of their family and filled my heart with their love.

I also give thanks to the Boulder Public Library's BoulderReads! It helped me learn how to read better and inspired me to try different things. It allowed me to feel good about myself.

I thank God for all the blessings I received.

* Names changed to protect their privacy.

Foreword

Janet Turner has been an inspiration to the staff, volunteers, and other adult learners of BoulderReads! at the Boulder Public Library. When she came to the program at the age of 69, her goal was to be able to read the Bible and to sing the hymns at church by reading the hymnal. Little did she know that she would reach those goals and many more, including writing her memoirs and reading more than 300 of the books in our literacy collection. Janet's willingness to work hard, her sense of humor, her way with words, her strong faith, and her rich life experience have made it a joy to know her. She always tells us how blessed she feels to be a part of BoulderReads! but it is the rest of us who have been blessed—by having Janet in our program. Janet's story is that of a strong woman who has not had an easy life, but rather than feeling sorry for herself or feeling resentful, Janet has always been determined to make the most of herself and be thankful for what she has. It has been a privilege to be part of her transformation from a nonreader to a published author.

Diana Sherry
Director, BoulderReads!

Introduction

My name is Janet Turner. I have been in Boulder, Colorado since 1986. I was born November 15, 1920, almost eight decades ago. I began my journey not knowing what direction I would take. I hope you'll come sit down and let me tell you my story.

I come from a family of 12 children. We were sharecroppers. Not much money, just a little schooling. I went through ninth grade and still couldn't read good. We worked from sunup till sundown. Trying to live by white man's rules, that's how it was in the South. We were told what to say, where to sit, where to eat and where to drink. The struggle was hard. With God's help, we survived.

In 1985, after my husband died, I looked around. I was all alone. I have one son, his wife and children. They live in Colorado. I moved to Boulder to live with them, not knowing no one but my family.

I always wanted to read better and understand what I read. So I got in the Boulder Public Library's BoulderReads! (formerly called Learning to Read Program). I learned that if you have the courage to reach out, someone will help you. I started at the second grade level and now I love books and I am writing short stories. They are mixed, from long ago and all between. Some are used in the *Discoveries* books published by BoulderReads!

People started telling me that I should put my stories together into a book. This is it! I thought to myself, if I could just get this book published I could give some of the funds to the Boulder Public Library. The night that idea was born I felt like I was running out of time; I can't use my right hand much now because of Parkinson's Disease.

I wrote some of these stories when I was still learning how to read; I wrote other ones much later. You will probably be able to tell, because some stories are very short and don't have much detail (those are the ones I wrote early on) and other stories are longer and have more detail. Some are written more in the way black people in the South talk (which is how I talk) and the ones I wrote later are more in Standard American English (which is the way most people in Colorado talk).

I am come to the end of my journey. I am getting slow. I hope and pray you have a chance to read my stories. You will find me somewhere along the way. I am the lady who went to look for her daddy by writing about him — and found herself.

Janet Turner
— the sharecropper's daughter

Welcome

You come in here and have a seat. I want to tell you a little about my life, 'cause I grew up in the South, black, poor; I couldn't read. Now, I'm almost 80, I can read now, I've had a good life, and I want to share my story. Maybe you'll want to hear it.

The Stories

When I Was Born

Long ago, on November 15, 1920, Lucy and James Driskell give birth to a little black baby girl. That was me. They brought me into this incredible world without giving me a choice. No one rolled out the red carpet. I was born on a birthing quilt on a very cold floor, bawling my eyes out. Someone wrapped me up in an old baby quilt and put me on the bed.

I was born on a farm in Eatonton, Georgia. Mom and Daddy named me Janet. When I was older, Mom told me about when she held me for the first time. She said I stopped crying and slowly looked in every corner of the room. If I looked at myself, I probably didn't like what I saw. I was long and straight, not much to look at.

As I think about when I was born, it's a good thing I didn't know what kind of life was ahead for me.

That's me playing softball at about age 17.

Our Lives Are a Gift of God: Not by Years, but One Day at a Time

*Are you comfortable? Would you rather sit over there?
I want to tell you about my family.*

God give our parents 12 children. I am the oldest. Then there is Jabe, Retha, Willie, Gertrude, Dorothy, Charlie, Harry, Jerry, Herman, Geneva and Catherine. I don't remember who started it, but 'most everyone had a nickname. I was "Shane," Retha was "Tiny," Willie was "Jim," Gertrude was "Gert," Dorothy was "Dot," Charlie was "Dick," Harry was "Hoony," Jerry was "Pete," Herman was "Junior" even though he wasn't really a junior, Geneva was "Eva" and Catherine was "Cat." Jabe wouldn't let us call him anything but Jabe. But my mother's sister, Erma, didn't have any children and she loved Jabe to pieces. She called him "Honey." It sounded like "Hoony" the way she said it. So all of us began calling him Hoony too. I guess that was like having a nickname.

We all was born in the South. We come in all shapes and sizes. We were just like stair steps, close and loving, and best friends. I won't try to describe my sisters and brothers, but if you saw one, you would know the rest. Some are short. Some tall. Some have dark skin like Daddy. Some are lighter like Mom. But we look alike in some way, mostly in our faces. Sometimes I scare myself when I look in the mirror. I see Tiny's face. I say, "What are you doing in the mirror?" Then I laugh.

By the time I was 12, I had seven brothers and sisters. I had so much work to do I had no time to play. I washed, cooked, sewed, cut wood, and did many other things. Mom didn't know how to sew except for maybe sewing up a quilt. So I taught myself. I did all the mending and sewing for my family. I used to make a pattern by laying whatever child I was sewing for down on a paper sack and drawing an outline of his body. Then I'd use the pattern to make him some clothes.

Mom taught my sisters how to make preserves and jellies for the family to eat. But I was so busy with sewing and my other chores that I never did learn how to make jams. Today, my sisters send me some for Christmas each year, because they know I don't know how to make it.

I wondered what the future held for my family, because I didn't want them to be like me. Mom was always working, so she didn't have time to talk with me. It would have been nice if someone had given me a little present all my own on a day that wasn't my birthday or Christmas. I was like a person who didn't exist. I felt like the world was passing me by.

My brother Jabe got a job to help out. My sister Tiny was the next child. She was gorgeous, charming, fun to be around. She loved to flirt, especially with someone else's boyfriend. If a boy came to see me, Tiny would take him. The sad thing is she didn't want him when she got him. And if he was crazy enough to follow her, I didn't want him back!

Tiny wanted no part of work. She knew how to get out of it, too. She would complain, "You know how much trouble I have with my stomach," and begin to cry, "Where's my daddy? I want my daddy." Daddy would show up and tell me when Tiny felt better she would help. When Daddy left, Tiny grumbled about the whole thing. "I told you all I wasn't going to work." We could have killed her.

We had a good life together as children and today we still have each other. Our lives are a gift of God, not by years, but one day at a time.

My mother in front of our house.

Life in the South

Have you ever thought about how people lived in the South a long time ago? Well, if you would like to know, walk along with me.

Daddy worked for two white brothers, Roy and Jimmy Johnson (names changed to protect privacy). A lot of black families worked for them. The Johnsons had a farm and a country grocery store, with Roy running the farm and Jimmy running the store.

People didn't have good homes to live in. The house I grew up in was in the country, southeast of Atlanta. The Johnsons owned it. It was in bad condition—floors and walls with cracks, a loft half without a ceiling, one window with no glass in, fireplace in every room, two lamps that burned kerosene, and water from the spring. It was heated with wood and it was cold in the winter.

The kitchen sat in a building separate from the house. It had a stove, but no refrigeration. We cooled things by hanging them in the well or putting them in the spring. There were ice boxes, but we had ice only on some weekends because you could only get it in a little town called Eatonton, about 12 miles away from our house. If we went to town, we asked our neighbors, "You want us to bring you back some ice?"

The only way of travel was by horse and wagon. We got our water from a well out in the yard. The water was good and cool. If we needed hot water, there was a place on the side of the stove where we heated water all day long.

The yard had no grass, just dirt and flowers. We swept the yard clean with a broom. For a long time, I didn't think you were supposed to have grass in a yard.

Daddy's boss didn't care how bad our house was. He did nothing about it. We couldn't get paint, so we used slick white or red clay to wash the walls of the house to make it look better. We found it under the banks of the nearby stream. We would dig out some white clay and mix it with water, then stir it up so the clay would dissolve. Then we dipped a rag in the clay mixture and washed down the walls on the inside and outside of our house. When they dried, they were white and clean. It lasted from one spring till the next.

I almost forgot to tell you about one of the most important things. We had no bathrooms. People used outhouses. On the porch or in the house, there was always a pitcher filled with water and a bowl for washing hands. We used a large tin tub for taking a bath in. It worked good. We got as clean as we wanted to.

Our family didn't have no money. So we used sacks to make clothes, bed things, sheets, dish cloths, just about everything we needed. Most everything came in sacking. The sacks was pretty—some flowered, some printed, some plain, some looked just like broadcloth.

All of us worked in the fields as soon as we was old enough. But when Mom and my sisters and I came home, we had to do the housework, laundry and cooking. *Would you like to sit and see how we made soap?* First, we built a fire out in the yard and put a pot over it. We put water and lye in the pot, then added some old grease saved from cooking bacon and hog meat. We stirred the pot constantly, bringing the soap to a boil, letting it simmer, then cool. Then we cut it into blocks. This soap was used for everything, including washing clothes and cleaning house.

When we needed barrels, we bought them from the Johnsons' store. Barrels were used to hold sugar, salt, pickles, pigs' feet and other things. *You see that barrel over there?* If you cut a barrel in half, you will have two tubs. We cleaned our clothes by washing them in tubs. We had a rubbing board cut out of wood. We washed heavy things, like towels and bed linens, once a week. We usually did this on Thursday or Friday, so everything would be clean for the weekend. We washed the children's clothes every other day. This took about two hours. White clothes were washed once in the barrel, then boiled in a pot, then washed again and rinsed. That also took about two hours. We didn't have clothespins, so we hung all the washed clothes over a rope to dry.

When there was washing, there was ironing. Mom ironed everything, even the rags. She said you could fold things better when they were ironed. Coal buckets were used to heat the irons. We made our own coal. First, we cut green pine wood into four-foot lengths, then dug a hole in the ground three feet deep. We built a fire in the hole. We took the wood and made a cut about a foot apart on each piece of wood. Then we put a layer of this wood on the fire, then a layer of damp sand, then more wood and more sand until it was three feet high. We let it slowly burn for about two or three weeks, then took the burnt logs out to cool. When they were cool, we broke them into pieces and stored them. When we wanted to iron, we used the pieces of coal to start a little fire in the bucket, then we put a piece of tin on top of the coals and put the iron on top of the tin to heat it up. We put a rag over the handle of the iron so we could hold it without getting burned.

A quilting frame hung down from the loft in the house. It was made from four pieces of wood held together with screws. We used it to make quilts from scraps of material taken from old clothes. First, we sewed the scraps together until they were as big as the quilting frame. Then, we made a lining for the quilt by sewing four big cotton sacks together. These sacks had held poison that was used to kill boll weevils in the cotton fields. They had been washed in lye and boiled in hot water. We hung the lining on the quilting frame. Then, we took some of the pretty, white cotton that we got from the cotton gin and put it on top of the lining. We put the quilt on top of the cotton and stitched it around the edge, so it would stay together. It was like a sandwich. We sewed it in rows, rolling it up so we could reach the other side, little by little.

We grew our own fruits and vegetables, then canned or dried them. For canning we washed and peeled the fruit and cut it up and put it on the stove in a big pan with just a little water and sugar. We let it cook for about 20 minutes, then took the clean jars and set them in a pan of water on the stove to boil. We put the hot fruit into the jars and if they was hot enough, they would seal.

For drying fruit you wash and peel them (or leave the peels on if you like it that way). Most people would have a table to do this on but our hen house was flat so we would lay a cloth on top to work on there. We have a thin piece of net to keep the bugs off the fruit. It would take about a month for the fruit to dry good and then we put it in sacks. People didn't keep their meat in the house but in smokehouses, and that is also where you hang your dried fruit. Since we didn't have candy and stuff, it's good to eat just the dried fruit. We also used some of it to make pickles, jellies, preserves and a lot more things. We also raised our own pigs, cows and chickens. When it was time to kill one or two hogs, the men in my family put a pen up on planks in the farmyard. The hogs were put in the pen to fatten up. All they had to do was eat. There was no room to walk around. When they got fat enough, the men built a big fire and put two or three huge kettles of water on to heat. It seemed like the pigs knew what was coming.

When the water boiled, a hole was made in the pen by knocking out some of the planks. As each one came out, the men would grab it, slit its throat and let it lay there for a few minutes to drain the blood. Then they'd hang it up by its back legs and slit it from its neck through its chest. It would hang there for about 15 or 20 minutes until most of its blood drained out. Then they took it down and cut its head off.

Hogs have lots of hair all over them. To get rid of the hair, the men slid the pig's body into the boiling water and made sure it got wet all over. The pig's head went in there afterwards, because it has hair too. The head and the feet were used to make "sow's" meat. We didn't let the pig stay in the water too long, because we didn't want it to cook. When we pulled it out, we took a big sharp butcher knife and scraped its hair off. It came off easily. We cut its feet off and put them back in the hot water for a while. When we took them out, we cut the hair off them, then removed the hooves. Taking off the hooves was like taking off a pair of shoes. We did the same thing with the pig's head.

Then, we split the pig's body wide open and removed the insides. We saved the liver, because we ate it along with the rest of the meat. The lungs, which we called "lights," were used for making "tom-tom." Tom-tom was made by cooking the lights and the liver together. When they were done, we mashed them up with vinegar, onions and cayenne pepper or whatever you wanted in it to make it taste good.

We rinsed the pig's bladder in warm water until it got clean. We always knew when it was clean enough because we could see through it like a piece of transparent paper. Then we took the tom-tom mixture and stuffed it into the bladder. We tied it up so the meat mixture wouldn't fall out. Then we hung it in the smokehouse until we wanted to eat it. The smokehouse had no floor, just the ground. It had a fire going all the time, but there was more smoke than fire.

We took the pig's intestines and squeezed the filth out of them. Then, we cleaned them in warm water until they were white. Mom used to soak them overnight. The next day, we had to scrape them and get everything out. The scraping makes them as thin as the plastic wrap everyone uses today. We cut the intestines into pieces about two feet long. These are called chitlins.

The pig was cut into six pieces: the two front shoulders, the two hams from its back, and the rest of the meat, which we cut into two pieces called the middlings. We trimmed the meat, separating the fat from the lean. We seasoned the scraps of lean meat with salt, pepper, sage or whatever we wanted to use, then put the mixture into a machine and ground it up. The strips of clean intestine were put on the end of the machine and the ground meat was forced into it. That's sausage. These were hung in the smokehouse too. Whenever you wanted some, you took however many lengths you wanted and fried them.

We put the pig fat and a little water into a pot out in the yard. The fire under the pot cooked the mixture. When the brown fat came to the top, we spooned it out. This was called cracklings. When the hot grease that was left in the pot cooled, it became as white as snow. This was lard. Some nights, we used some of the crackling to make homemade crackling bread. We ate it with buttermilk. It was a delicious meal.

The rest of the meat was packed into a wooden box of salt, one piece at a time. The salt draws all the water out of it. Two or three weeks later, we heated another pot of water. We dipped the meat into the boiling water just long enough to get the salt off. Then we laid it on a table and used some cotton sacks to dry it real good. We fixed a mixture of lard, brown sugar syrup, salt, pepper, sage, basil and any spices we wanted, then covered the meat with it. We put it in a flour sack to keep any bugs off it, tied it up and hung it up in the smokehouse.

The best part of a hog is the tenderloin meat along the spine. We usually saved it as a treat for our family and any neighbors who helped slaughter the pig. In the country, everyone helped each other and we all shared in the meat.

We had cows, so we had to milk them. *Stand here and watch.* First, we washed the cow's bag. We carried a bucket, then set it under the cow's bag and milked the cow. Sometimes the cows were mean and we had to be careful not to get kicked.

We took the milk to the house and strained it into a churn. Then we waited about a day for the milk to get thick. This is called clabber. When the milk got to be clabber, we churned it with a dasher. The dasher had a paddle on one end that went into the churn. The other end went through the lid of the churn. We moved the dasher up and down until butter came to the top. We took it out, washed it and added salt. Then it was ready to eat. What was left in the churn was buttermilk.

We had lots of chickens. We ate them and their eggs. Selling chickens and eggs was easy. You know chickens just run around in the yard and we never ate the ones that ran around in the yard because they would eat everything. (Some people don't mind what chickens eat, but we did!) The ones we were going to eat had to be kept in a pen off the ground. You kill them by chopping the heads off and then you prepare them the same way as the pigs, but the water shouldn't be as hot. You put them in the water and the feathers just come off so easy.

To get eggs, you go to the chicken house or the yard where the hens have their nests. They lay the eggs and then just wander off and in the evening we would go gather the eggs. Sometimes they would just be on the ground. Our hens had nests all over the place and sometimes the eggs would hatch before we'd find them and little babies would be running around.

Have you ever seen sugar cane? It grows in the fields and we made syrup out of it. We took the cane to a mill and put the cane in it. Then the owner hitched his mule up to the mill and when the mule walked around the mill it would turn a stone that crushed the cane. This squeezed the juice out of the cane. The juice went through a pipe to one or two pots. There was a fire burning under the pots and the heat cooked the juice into syrup. Sometimes we just drank some of the juice as it came out. When it's cold, it's good. We paid for the use of the mill with syrup.

Most of our neighbors lived about half a mile from us. Some of them kept to themselves, but the rest of us shared everything with each other. There wasn't much to do in the country, so getting together to share food and help each other was fun. That's the way country folk survived, by helping each other.

Would you like to have some lunch? I think you would like the food. When I lived on the farm, a typical lunch was fried chicken, boiled potatoes or rice, a vegetable like green beans or sliced tomatoes, a bowl of fruit, and cornbread muffins with jelly or preserves. We drank homemade lemonade or buttermilk. Dessert was tea cakes and they were delicious.

You getting tired? No? Okay, I'll keep talking. I is enjoying your visit.

My Worst Nightmare

It seemed like I was doing all the work and I got tired of it. My sisters were too young to help and my brothers were lazy. They didn't do much of anything to help around the house. And every time I turned around, there was a new baby and I had to stay home to take care of it.

So when my mother told me to do something, I wouldn't always do it right away. I was hardheaded. I just wanted to do what I wanted to do. And sometimes I forgot what she'd told me to do.

Well, Mom got tired of it. One morning, she asked me to get something from the trunk where we kept the boys' clothes. I truly forgot to do it. That evening, I remembered what she'd asked. I ran to get it out of the trunk. I put my head down in the trunk, looking for what I was supposed to get. All of a sudden, I was standing on my head in the trunk!

Unknown to me, Mom had been watching me all day, waiting to see when I'd get around to doing what she'd asked. When I finally looked in the trunk, she grabbed my legs and lifted both of them up in the air. It scared me and made me lose my balance. I didn't know what was happening. I thought the world had come to an end. Then, she spanked me with an old shoe with tacks in the heel.

I never forgot again.

The Good Old Days

Welcome to the good old days in the late 1920s.

No machines. Everything done by hand. Blacks had no money. We were treated awful, like wild animals. We had to look up to the white man like he was our king. The Johnsons were as poor as the blacks. The only difference was they could get loans from banks. But no bank would loan money to blacks.

Roy and Jimmy wanted us to plant cotton. That's where the money come from. They was always talking us into clearing new land. They said we would make more money. I didn't see no more. Neither did my family. More work and no pay. Every detail about cotton was hard. I never liked raising it. God knows I tried.

Winter, we had wood to cut, hogs and cows to kill, new fields to clear for planting. Clearing land meant cutting down trees, digging up roots, moving rocks and turning over land. After we cut trees and roots, did rocking, and turned over land, we cleaned up the lot and spread animal droppings all over the field, then plowed the land again. Then it was ready to plant. We was busy the whole year. Our work was never done.

We planted in spring. First, we opened the row up by plowing. The plow was pulled by a mule. Next, we put fertilizer in and the cotton seeds on top of it. We covered the seeds with some soil. Then, we prayed for rain. If it rained, the cotton came up soon. If it didn't rain, we had to start all over again.

While we waited for the cotton to grow, we planted our own garden. It was close to the house. We planted corn, peanuts, sweet potatoes and other things. We worked all summer picking cotton, digging potatoes and peanuts, pulling corn. By the time we caught our breath, the cotton needed thinning out with a hoe. When we finished that, there was grass everywhere in the cotton fields. We got it out with a hoe, then plowed the middle of the row out. That left a trench for the water. The cotton sat up higher than the trench. That way the roots wouldn't rot from sitting in water.

The cotton grew fast. There was insects called boll weevils. They eat holes in the cotton bolls if you ain't careful. If they got on our cotton and we didn't know it, they would kill our crop in a few days. We had to watch out for them, and if they came, we had to put poison dust in a sack, go to the field in the morning while the dew is on the cotton, then shake the poison dust all over the cotton. And all over us. I don't remember what kind of poison it was, but it went right through our clothes. Sometimes, if we kept the dusty clothes on too long, we could feel the poison burning our skin. It was important to get the clothes off as quick as you could. When we came in from the field in the morning, we used a tin tub to bathe in. But there was no way we could get all that poison off. When I think about all the dust that was left on our bodies, it makes me sick.

Daddy thought he knew what he was doing by not saying anything to the boss. But I think he was fooling himself. He had to depend on the white man for work. I did understand, but it seemed like it was always in the white man's favor. Daddy did all the work and never had anything to show for it. The white man got all the money.

We began picking the cotton in August. The cotton bolls was white as snow. That's the way we wanted them to be. They was fresh and heavy. We got more for a pound that way, because it weighed more. Men and women picked a lot of cotton in a day. Daddy could pick 500 pounds. But I knew people who picked 600 or 700 pounds each day. We prayed it don't rain and for our cotton to stay clean.

Cotton seeds come in burlap sacks. We used the sacks when we picked the cotton. We made them any size we wanted. We folded the top of the sack down and made a strap from part of the sack, then put the strap from one side to the other side, like a shoulder bag. We put one arm through the strap and over our head. Some liked the sack long, so they could drag it on the ground.

We also used the seed sacks to collect the cotton. We did this by taking four sacks, opening them up, then sewing them all together into a big sheet. Then, when our sacks got full of cotton, we emptied them out onto the sheet. We put one sheet in the middle of where we were picking cotton and one on each side, so we wouldn't have to walk so far to empty our sacks.

When we was ready to take our cotton to the cotton gin, we put up the sides around the wagon and poured our cotton into it. In one wagon, we could put enough cotton to make two bales.

The man who ran the gin was a good friend of Daddy's boss. Before we got the cotton weighed, Roy and the gin man took some of our cotton and set it aside. They took some from every black that went there. I say they stole it. The gin owner ginned our cotton by using a mule or horse to turn the gin. Then he baled it and sacked the seeds. We paid the gin man with cotton or seeds, whatever he wanted. Roy was there to get paid some of his money that we owed him. That didn't leave us very much.

I felt so sorry for my parents at that minute. Daddy was Roy's footstool and I didn't like it. I wished I could stand in my Daddy's shoes, so I could tell Roy off. But I wouldn't last a day, not even a minute. Daddy thought if we said anything we would get in trouble. And he was right. He knew us better than we knew ourselves. Daddy wore his shoes well. He was a good man. Every time I talk about him or write about him, I learn things I never knew.

Some people say I didn't find the good old days good at all. But the good old days are where my roots are. We was blessed in many ways. All the years we was growing up, we was hardly ever sick and never in trouble. *I hope you understand what I mean.*

Thank you, Lord.

This is my cousin's truck which was used to haul cotton in.

This was the barbecue stand behind the church.
Twice a year we'd have a big meeting and these guys
would bring their truck and sell ice cream and barbecue.

Big Mama

You got grandparents? Are they still alive?

We called my grandmother Big Mama. I was nine years old when she died. When I think how nice she was, I feel good. I remember some things about her. I used to look up and see her coming down the road. She would be wearing a long, black dress and a crisp, white apron that almost covered her dress. In her hand was a basket filled with good things to eat—bread, tea cakes, jellies and other things she had made. She didn't have money for gifts. Anyway, the store was too far away. That basket was filled with love. That is what I loved most about her.

Big Mama grew up in Georgia. Most of her sisters and brothers went north when they grew up. After her children were grown, she would go visit them. She would bring little gifts back and tell us about the North, places she went, things she saw and all about our cousins.

My granddaddy died when I was five or six, so I spent more time with Big Mama. She cared for the neighbors when they were sick or in need of help. I would help her carry soup, milk, butter and eggs to them. I couldn't do much work, but I made little quilts and doll clothes from scraps that she had.

Big Mama loved church. It was fun going to church—walking, talking and sometimes singing. It made no difference if it was cold or raining, we walked. Her favorite prayers were, "The Lord will make a way" and "I thank God for everything." At the time, I didn't know what she meant. As I grew up, I saw how true those words were.

My grandmother taught me a lot—how to love God, go to church, help someone along the way. I remember the good times we shared. I'm glad I got to know her.

This is my grandmother;
we called her Big Mama.

In Those Days, You Could Not Afford to Get Sick

You ever been sick? You ever thought about what might happen if you couldn't see a doctor? Let me tell you.

We lived a long way from a doctor. Travel was difficult, and even if one lived next door we couldn't afford it. If you was black, you had to have money. So Mom did what had been handed down through generations: home remedies.

Herbs was found in the woods and some was used for medicine. Rubbing salve was made from tallow. Sassafras was the herb we used for hot tea or cold tea. Hot tea was good for children's diseases like chicken pox, mumps, measles and other things. It made us break out faster. Rabbit tobacco is an herb. We used it for tea and smoking tobacco.

There was no way to take temperatures. The only way Mom knew I had a fever was that I got hot. If I had one, she wrapped me up in peach leaves or rubbed me down with alcohol or put me in a tub of cold water. When Mom needed a bandage, she cut up sheets and used the strips for bandages.

When Mom had a baby, she used a midwife to help her. The midwife was like a doctor in many ways. She would stay a day or two if things were bad. People didn't have much money. If we had money, we paid. If not, we gave whatever we had.

There was no dentist in the country. We cleaned our teeth most times with soda or salt. When our teeth hurt, there wasn't much we could do for it. It was bad not having a dentist.

I got burned once when I was nine. I was standing with my back to the fire in the fireplace. I pulled up my nightgown to get warm, just like a grown-up, and it caught on fire. By the time I found out what was happening, my nightgown was burning good. I ripped the gown off and stamped the fire out. But one of my legs got burned and it drew up. For a long time I couldn't walk. I didn't go to a doctor. I had no medicine for pain. I cried and I prayed. I didn't think I would walk again. But I did.

In those days, you could not afford to get sick.

Where Babies Come From

Mothers used to be sly with their children. If you asked them to tell you something, they was so secret. They made something up. I went down that path.

When Mom was carrying one of her babies, I didn't know we were going to have one. Everyone's mom was a little fat, so I thought that's what was happening. Before the baby came, we cleaned the house and the yard, washing everything. Mom didn't know how to sew, so she never made baby clothes. But somehow, they were always ready. Later, I learned that Big Mama made them for each new baby.

When it was nearly time for delivery, sheets, quilts and towels were laid on a table so they'd be ready to use. Nearby was a chair. When Mom was in labor, the quilts were folded and put on the floor. A sheet was put on top of the quilts. Then the chair was put on top of the sheet. Mom kneeled down on the quilts, resting her arms on the chair. There was a big fire in the fireplace and in the stove. A pan of hot water was on the stove.

Daddy would get the wagon and go to get the lady they called a midwife. She was a little old black lady with a black satchel in her hand. I never knew what was in that satchel, but I knew a baby was coming soon because we never saw her until a baby was on the way. If it was in the daytime, the children went to Big Mama's. If it was at night, we was asleep and stayed home. When we got back from Big Mama's or woke up, a new baby was there.

When I was older, I needed to know certain things. If I asked my parents, they wouldn't tell me the whole truth. That confused me more. Once, I asked Mom where did babies come from. She smiled and said, "They come from a rotten tree stump." For a long time, every time I passed one I would look for a baby.

I believed what Mom told me, because she said so. I finally learned otherwise by putting two and two together. But it wasn't until I was grown that I knew the whole truth.

Struggling to Survive

Do you love your parents?
Do you think about all the things they do for you?

My daddy was a good, kind, caring man, and fun to be around. He was tall and thin with brown skin, black curly hair and sad black eyes. He wore overalls, a blue shirt, brown boots and a big hat. He loved playing with the children. His special game was baseball.

It was bad in the South from 1918 through 1930. Daddy worked hard every day, from sunup till sundown. Most of the blacks, including us, had no money or land. So we sharecropped. Daddy borrowed money from the Johnsons to grow a crop that he then shared with them. But at the end of the year, our share of the crop went to the Johnsons to pay our debt. So we borrowed all over again for the next year.

At Jimmy's store, you could charge most anything. We had our own milk and butter, and Mom made soap for laundry and cleaning the house. But we bought sugar, flour and spices at the store. Everything was so expensive that Mom sold eggs, chickens and pigs to help buy the things we needed. At the end of the year, the Johnsons told us what we owed them. We never got receipts, so we didn't know how much we spent. We never saw what they put in their book. We never got ahead. They wanted us to work all the time then they took everything. We never had anything to show for all the work we did. The Johnson brothers owned us.

As my brothers and sisters growed up, we tried to change things. We asked Daddy to get a receipt. He said no one else gets one. It would just start trouble and he was afraid of what might happen.

Mom was the strong one. She was light-complexioned, black hair, black eyes. She was a small, unique lady. Mom knew how to survive and make ends meet. It made no difference how hard the struggle was, so we thought. But beneath the long dress and the white apron, she was just Mom, who raised her children all day and put them to bed at night. And when she thought they was asleep, she prayed for strength. We could hear her crying late in the night.

Mom went to church and took us with her. Her good rubbed off on her children. She didn't have to go looking for them at night. That was one trouble she didn't have.

Daddy and Mom was good together. He give us some of the things we needed and she give us the rest. They had only a little education, but they had dreams. They just never came true.

You might not see it now, but when you grow up, you'll appreciate your parents, the way I do now.

Namesake

Do you know where your name came from?
I do. Mine came from my great aunt.

My mother, Lucy, was one of seven children: Willie, J.P., John, Gene, Erma, Dave and Mom. Erma and Mom were the only girls. Daddy just had a half-brother, Will. None of us, including Daddy, knew about him until we were grown up. My brother Jabe found out about him. When he told his boss his last name was Driskell, the man asked if he knew Will Driskell. Jabe said no. Then he went looking for Will and found him. Will had three boys: Jessy, William and "Spudge."

Daddy's Aunt Janet and her husband, Uncle Nap, lived down the road from where we lived. We pronounced her name as if it was Janette. Aunt Janet was my great-aunt. I was her namesake. But she never acted like I was anything special. She never gave me anything, such as cookies or homemade candies.

Aunt Janet was a large lady. Weighed about 250 pounds. She wasn't very tall. She had dark eyes and dark skin. She mostly wore a long dress and a crisp white apron. She always looked neat and clean. I never saw her hair because she wore a scarf around her head. She always had on makeup. She wore too much and it was too white, as if she had white flour on her face. It looked funny.

Aunt Janet was a proud black lady. She and I weren't close. I never went down there by myself for a visit. She had no children of her own and she wasn't a friendly person. She treated us like we were little rats running around. She acted like she didn't want us to touch her, because we might get her dirty. We didn't always have good clothes or shoes. Sometimes no shoes at all. I think Aunt Janet thought we weren't good enough for her. Or maybe she just didn't like children.

Once, Mom got sick. Aunt Janet brought some food. She was all dressed up. A pretty tea towel covered the food. The food was just for Mom, not the children or Daddy. But after Aunt Janet left, Mom gave the food to the children. She thought we needed it more.

Aunt Janet must have been a very lonely person. Uncle Nap would have the neighborhood down to their house in late summer for a watermelon eating. That was the only time we would all be down there at the same time.

One day when Uncle Nap was at work, Aunt Janet wandered off in the woods. She couldn't find her way back home. Men looked for her all night. They didn't find her until the next morning. After that, she was afraid of everyone.

A few months later, she died. All of us went to her funeral service. It was held in her front yard. We buried her in the cemetery across the road from her house. The grave doesn't have a slab on it, just a big rock for the headstone. When I go home, I like to stop at the cemetery and put flowers on her grave.

Funerals

There were no funeral homes to take care of people when they died. So when someone died, their family and neighbors gather to take care of the body. They heat some water in a big old pot and bathe the deceased. They put clean clothes on him and dress him.

They put two planks across a couple of chairs and put a sheet over the planks. This is called a cooling board and the body is laid on it. Then someone takes the wagon and goes to town, gets a casket, brings it home and puts the body in it.

The night before the funeral, everyone stays up all night—eating, drinking, singing and talking. Some people go stand by the casket and say goodbye. Some just stand there and look. People tell lots of stories about the deceased and memories are shared.

The day of the funeral, the neighbors bring in more food for lunch. Funeral services are always held in the morning. The casket is put in a wagon. Horses pull it to the cemetery beside the highway. A graveside service is held. A rock is placed at the head of the grave. After the funeral, everyone goes back to the house and eats lunch.

The Bell

*You ever thought about if you didn't have no phone?
What about an emergency? How would you tell people?
Let me tell you about our bell.*

Bells were used for many things. We had one in our yard. What I remember most about it is how the bell was so high up on a pole. There was a rope hanging down from it. We pulled the rope up and down. That's what made the bell ring.

The bell carried messages all across the countryside. It was the fastest way to get a message out. In the country, the bell rang at 12 noon. That meant the sun was high in the sky and it was time for the field workers to come home for dinner. When the bell rang fast, that meant something was wrong. Maybe someone died or was sick. I remember when my granddaddy's house was on fire they rang the bell. It was so sad.

Some people said they could tell by the sound of the bell if the news was good or bad. Sometimes the bell scared people. When it rang, people came running from all around. The bell was a way of life.

Determined

I hope you know how to swim.

    I grew up determined. I believed in myself. In my case it wasn't always so good. There was a creek on our farm. Sometimes we had to cross it on a log. I wanted to cross so I could go swimming. We thought walking in the creek was swimming.
    When I was 12, I wanted to go fishing. People said it was fun. But I was scared of worms and live fish. Mom didn't fish and Daddy didn't have time to take me.
    One day, Daddy felt sorry for me and he took me fishing. We went to the creek on the farm. I caught a big fish. Daddy showed me how to bring him in. Then, my foot slipped and I fell in the creek and lost the fish. I thought I was drowning, but Daddy got me out.
    I never wanted to go fishing again.
    I am afraid of heights and the creek was deep. I kept asking Daddy to take me across. One day he decided to do it. I was so scared.
    Daddy went across and said, "It's all right. Come on."
    I began to cry and pray all at the same time. I closed my eyes. I could hear the sound of the water running by. I felt dizzy. I tried again. My feet started slipping. Finally, I got down and crawled across.
    I never did learn how to swim.

Going to School

Let me tell you about school.

Where we lived was called Flat Rock. It was what we called our neighborhood, not a real town. Where the two streets crossed, there was a grove of trees on one corner, the Johnsons' store on another, our school on another, and the Flat Rock Primitive Baptist Church on the other. The Johnson brothers each had a house near this crossroad. Our neighbors lived half a mile away in any direction.

It was about three miles from where we lived on the Johnson farm to the one-room school. Kids came from all directions. We had to walk about 45 minutes to get there. We prayed for the weather to be good, because we couldn't go if it was bad.

Daddy's boss tried to find things for us to do just to keep us out of school. When we had to help with the farm, we couldn't go to school. Roy didn't want us to have an education. He and Jimmy didn't have much, and I think they didn't want us to know more than they did. We stayed home from school about as many days as we went.

There were about 20 to 25 students. They were all from the neighborhood. Some were poor and others were better off. The ones who wore nice clothes usually got them from relatives who had moved north and sent them some nice used clothing. We carried our lunch to school.

The school was heated by a wood-burning stove. People gave wood, but they couldn't always get the wood to the school or find the time to bring it in. Sometimes it got so cold inside. School usually started at nine o'clock. But some kids had to feed animals at home and get in wood. So we waited around for them to get there.

We didn't always have a teacher. When we did, she couldn't read much better than the students. The teacher divided us into small groups. Then she'd go around to each group to teach us. We had just a few books at school and none to take home. There just weren't enough to go around. So we didn't have any homework to do or any books to read for fun.

I loved school. But I went through ninth grade and still couldn't read good. I was always sorry about that.

Do you know how to read? You just better keep on reading and getting better. You don't know how lucky you are. If you don't read good, keep tryin' to learn! It's so important!

Christmas at School

Do you celebrate Christmas?

Christmas at school was lots of fun. Two weeks before the holiday came, we was busy. We gathered some holly that had red berries, then decorated the school with it. We used evergreen branches to make a wreath for the front door and hung mistletoe.

We cut down a tree from the nearby woods. Then we made Christmas ornaments, snowmen and a big star for the top of the tree. Most of the paper we used for the decorations came from the pages of an old Sears & Roebuck catalog. We made chains out of different colored paper and made glue from flour and water to hold the chains together.

Nobody else could sew, so I made little rag dolls and stuffed animals for Santa Claus to give to the children. I also made costumes for Santa Claus, the three Wise Men and the baby Jesus. Some of the children brought in cookies and candy. We put the handmade gifts in Santa Claus' bag.

In December 1934, on the last day of school for the year, we had a program for our parents. My brother Jabe, 12, dressed up as Santa Claus. Some children were the Wise Men. Others played Mary, Joseph and the baby Jesus. We sang lots of Christmas songs. Then Santa Claus passed out the gifts from his bag. We played games and ate the picnic lunch the parents had brought.

After the program and lunch was over, we were a little sad because all the decorations had to come down. We put the ones from the tree in boxes and passed them around to the children to choose one at a time until they were all gone.

The children was happy about how good everything turned out. They had given of themselves the best way they knew how when they took part in the program and helped make the decorations. Giving is what Christmas is all about. *Don't you think so too?*

Church

Do you go to church?
Church has always been real important to me.

My parents, grandparents and great-grandparents all went to the Flat Rock Primitive Baptist Church near Flat Rock Creek in Putnam County, Georgia. The church was small. It was heated with a big-belly stove and they got water from the spring. The neighbors built the church and kept it up. They built benches and tables. People could always use it for a meeting place, but not at night. There was no electricity.

I grew up around that church. My school was across the road from it. They didn't believe in Sunday School or musical instruments. They had no choir. The whole congregation sang hymns. One hymn I loved best of all, "A Charge to Keep I Have a God to Glorify."

Primitive Baptist's baptism service was more beautiful than anything. They baptized in the creek early in the morning. The creek was down the road from the church. It had flat rocks all the way across. You could stand on them and take your shoes off. Some places the water ran over the rocks. The middle of the creek was a perfect place for baptizing. But they didn't believe in young children joining the church. If you was still living at home with your parents, you wasn't old enough. That made me sad. I never did understand.

No church had service every Sunday, so I visited other churches too. When I was 18, I felt like I was a good enough person and close enough to God to join a church. But since I was living with Mom and Daddy, I still couldn't join the Primitive Baptist. So I decided to join another nearby Baptist church.

One Sunday night, along with 15 or 20 others, I went to church and put on a long white gown and wrapped a white sheet around it. We were put in a little room at the side of the pulpit. When it was time, we went down some steps into the church. The baptizing pool was located beneath the pulpit. The reverend and a deacon was waiting for us. When it was my turn, the reverend dipped me in the water. I was scared to death. I was afraid I'd drown, but I was also scared

This is the front of the Flat Rock Primitive Baptist Church where I went as a child.

This is the creek where people were baptized. There were flat rocks right out in the middle that you could stand on.

they weren't going to let me join if I didn't do it. And I didn't think I'd be a whole person in God's sight unless I was. I made out fine and when it was over I was very happy.

I love the Flat Rock Primitive Baptist Church. It looks today like it did then. It never changes. They still don't allow children to join. I try to go back once a year to hear a good service and see the people I grew up with. I always feel good when I go there. Out of all the churches I've been to, it is my favorite.

This is the altar and pulpit of the church.

The Gathering

During the 1930s, the fourth Sunday in August was a big day at the Flat Rock Primitive Baptist Church. Most all of the crops had been gathered. It was a time when most people took a little vacation. They would gather to eat and have fun. Everyone would be there.

Everyone wanted to drink, but they couldn't because they were meeting at the churchyard. No one had land to use for the gathering. Mom's Aunt Anna had a big place. We went there for a while. But that didn't work. It just wasn't convenient.

An old white man lived in the neighborhood. The only family he had was some distant cousins. They thought he was a bum and didn't pay him any attention. Most of the man's neighbors were black. They took care of him by sharing food with him. Mom used to give him soup and other foods she knew he'd like. She also offered to take care of his laundry for him.

When the man heard about our problem, he gave us some land down by the creek. It had trees and a pond on it. After cleaning it up, it turned out to be pretty. Then someone gave an old house. The men built a shed out of it. Tables, benches and grills were built. A hole was dug in the ground for the barbecue pit. The gathering day was changed to a Saturday. Everything was ready.

That morning, the neighborhood was up early getting ready to go. Some walked. Some rode in wagons. Our friends and people from other neighborhoods came. Most all of the black families that went north came back for that day. They were dressed up in clothes like we never seen before. What we didn't know was that their clothes were rented because the people were having a hard time. They couldn't afford to buy new things. Now, we talk and laugh about the good and bad times so long ago.

When we first got to the shed, we would have a prayer meeting—singing, praying and giving thanks to the Lord for the summer and everyone coming together one more time. After breakfast, the ladies put the things they had made from cotton sacks out on the tables. Sugar, flour, meal and fertilizers came in white cloth sacks. When the sacks were bleached to get the letters out they looked like

This is where the Gathering took place. The land was donated for it.

broadcloth. Other sacks were printed with flowers, plaids, stripes or with patterns that children like. The ladies made beautiful things out of these sacks—skirts, jackets, shirts, slacks, tablecloths, bed linens, children's clothes and rugs. Homemade soap, candies, canned fruits, vegetables and jellies were put out on the tables too. All of these things were for sale. This was a way the ladies had to make some money.

After eating lunch, which the older children prepared, everyone did different things. The younger children took naps. The men hitched two mules to a wagon and drove the wagon down by the shed. The ladies would fix a bed in the wagon for the babies and small children to sleep on. The children loved the wagon. Some of the ladies would stay with them so they wouldn't fall out.

The older children played all kinds of games. We played baseball, hopscotch, ring-around-the-rosy, spin the ball, and card games. Daddy taught us everything he knew about cards. We learned how to play Blackjack, Whist, Setback and Five Up. *Do you know how to play any of these games?* Our "money" was peanuts and corn, and we played for blood! Mom called it gambling. She didn't like it at all.

The men started barbecuing three pigs early in the morning. They were cooked with hickory wood. After lunch, a fire was built around a big pot that sat up on rocks. The men fried chicken in the pot. The ladies prepared the other food at home—vegetables, salads, breads and desserts. Everything smelled so good!

I remember one dessert so well. It was called butter roll. No recipe. This is the way I made it. One cup sugar, one-half cup butter, three cups milk, two teaspoons vanilla, two pie crusts. Put the milk, half-cup of the sugar, three tablespoons butter and the vanilla in a pot. Bring it to a boil, then set it aside. Roll out the pie crust and cut it into five-inch squares. Use the sugar and butter you have left and put it on the squares. Fold the corners of each square to the middle and pinch them together. Put them in a greased baking dish. Bake them in a 350-degree oven for 20 minutes or until the squares get brown. Take them out of the oven and pour the hot milk mixture over them. Put the dish back in the oven for 20 minutes more. It tastes just like warm vanilla ice cream. *Want me to make you some?*

In the cool of the evening, before we had our big meal, lanterns were hung. We would hold hands, pray and sing, and thank the Lord for the good day. Some would cry, some looked happy, some looked sad, some just talked. I asked my Mom what was going on. She said, "You just keep on living. You'll find out."

After eating, a special game was played: fireball. A rag ball was soaked in kerosene and lit. Six men wearing gloves threw the ball to each other. It was so pretty.

Then it was time to go home. The fire was put out. The lanterns were taken down. We gave thanks to God and we all went home.

Getting into Trouble

Have you ever done something your parents told you not to do? Let me tell you about when I did.

It made no difference how large or how little a place, wherever you planted watermelons, it was called a patch. Daddy planted a watermelon patch every year. He told us he didn't care how big the watermelons got, we couldn't pull them until the Fourth of July. They wouldn't be ripe until then.

But we knew when they were ripe. We didn't think Daddy knew what he was talking about. Waiting to pick them until the Fourth of July was just an old saying he'd been saying for a long time. Sometimes the watermelons got too ripe when you waited until then.

Three days before the holiday, Jabe and I decided to check them out. I was 14 and Jabe was 12. We went to the patch. Jabe carried a knife. He plugged ten of the biggest watermelons by cutting a little piece out to see was it ripe down inside. After he plugged each melon, I stuck the pieces back. We finally busted one open right in the middle of the patch and ate it. Then we went home.

Daddy happened to come by the patch that same day. I guess he was checking the melons out for the holiday, not thinking we did something to them. He saw somebody had busted this one melon in the middle of the patch. He got curious. He started looking at all of his prize watermelons, the big ones. And he found out they'd been plugged.

He went home and asked Jabe and me if we had been to the watermelon patch. I think he was hoping it would be someone else, because he had told us they wouldn't be ripe yet. When we told him we did it, he said, "You knew they wouldn't be ripe until the Fourth of July!" Daddy was hurt because we didn't obey him. Jabe got the whipping of his life. I cried the whole time because I thought I should have gotten whipped too, even if I wasn't the one who plugged the watermelons.

A few weeks later, Mom was out and Daddy was working in the field somewhere. My sisters and brothers and I were getting ready to go to the watermelon patch. This time, Daddy told us it was okay. Just before we left, some people came by the house with some samples of tobacco and snuff for Daddy to try. They gave it to us to give to Daddy, then left. We opened the tobacco and chewed some on the way to the patch. We thought we were so grown up. We didn't know you were supposed to spit it out, so we just swallowed it.

When we got to the patch, we began to get sick. We picked some watermelon and started back for home. But we were so sick, we started falling down, busting some of the melons. We lay down by the side of the road, too sick to move. I've never been so sick in my life.

Daddy got home, found the tobacco open and came looking for us. He knew exactly what happened. When he found us, he carried us home, one at a time, and put us to bed. We were sick for days.

That was one time we didn't get punished for what we did. Daddy said we had been punished enough.

I Made a Promise to Daddy

Do people sometimes treat you bad?

Growing up can be awful, especially in the South during the Depression. The struggle was hard for whites and blacks. They had to fight to survive. The whites needed the work done and the blacks needed jobs. Somewhere in between, they had to depend on each other.

Daddy's bosses, Roy and Jimmy, didn't like blacks. In fact they hated them. As far as they were concerned, we couldn't possibly think for ourselves. They said anything they wanted to us. Sometimes it hurt so bad I wanted to talk back. Sometimes I wanted to yell loud just to see what would happen to me.

But Daddy taught me an important way of living. He said there were rules. I wasn't to walk off when white people were talking to me and I wasn't to talk back to them. They don't like it when blacks talk back. He said, "If you have to open your mouth, just sing. I know you'll sing so loud they'll walk away." I promised him that's what I would do.

One day, when I was in my teens, I stopped by Jimmy's store. Some white people were sitting around. I was just a stick then, tall and thin. Jimmy said, "You need weights on your head to stop you from growing." His friends laughed. They thought it was so funny. But I was mad.

I looked at him and half grinned. I asked him did he know anything about weights. He said yes. I said, "That's a surprise. I didn't know you knew anything!" Everyone stopped laughing.

I walked out of the store. My mouth had got me in trouble. I knew I should have thought before I had spoke. I had gone too far. I thought, Lord, what have I done. I wondered how I could tell Daddy that I had broken my promise.

When I got home, I was trembling all over. I told Daddy everything that was said. He asked, "Why didn't you just leave?" I didn't know what to say. I didn't have an answer, because I knew he was right.

I was so scared. Jimmy and Roy belonged to a group of white people called night riders. They rode horses at night and usually covered their faces. They did things to blacks to keep them under control. They would come to a black's house and take him to the woods and hang him. Nothing was done about it. The group Jimmy and Roy belonged to was so bad they never hid their faces. They didn't care if we knew who they were. I knew that if anything bad happened to my family, it would be because of me.

I had nightmares for a long time. But nothing happened and I thanked the Lord.

Standing Up to People

Roy and Jimmy used to say anything they wanted to my family and our friends. They treated us so bad. They thought blacks were alone, but we always had God. We just started praying and singing, and they would leave.

One day, it rained hard. It was so wet we couldn't go out that evening. I was sitting on the doorstep polishing my nails when Roy, Daddy's boss, came by. He stopped and asked, "Gal, what are you doing?"

Before I could answer, Daddy came out of the house and asked who was he talking to. He said, "That gal." When Daddy got through telling him off, he went around telling people my Daddy was crazy. The Johnsons thought if you had good sense you wouldn't talk back. Daddy thought what he did was all right. He got his point over. The boss was nice after that.

Another time, I was on my way home. Roy came slouching across the field. He said, "Hi, gal." I kept on walking. He screamed so loud I stopped. He said, "You heard me."

I said, "My name's not gal. My name is Janet." I kept on walking. I had to stop myself from saying something else back to him.

Only sometimes I forgot.

No Respect for Blacks

When I think about the time we spent on Roy's and Jimmy's farm, I feel sad. The Johnsons had no respect for blacks. They cheated them and did everything they could to keep them in their place. They were just plain old jim crow. Jimmy was the worst. He looked evil. Some say he was rotten to the core. He planted little doubts in some of the blacks' minds to get them mad at each other.

The Johnsons went in and out of some of the blacks' houses like they lived there. Those blacks were treated better. Roy and Jimmy would take any black women they wanted. Jimmy was the father of at least two black boys. But the blacks were afraid of them. They thought they might lose their jobs or that Roy and Jimmy would send in the night riders. They had no power.

Daddy told Roy and Jimmy he didn't want them in our house. He didn't allow that. That surprised them. They thought Daddy would be too scared to stand up for himself and his family. They told him he was taking a big chance when he talked back to them.

When I was a teenager, I got curious about why some of our neighbors were treated better. But when I asked questions, I got no answers. One day, I asked Daddy again.

Daddy said, "Maybe they're treated better because they don't talk back to the boss like you do."

I knew it wasn't true. I told him, "I heard you talking back to them once!"

He replied, "That's because I'm the Daddy and you're the child. I only say things when they push me too far. That's why they call me crazy."

Later, I found out why those blacks let Roy and Jimmy stay with them. I worked with some black women who thought kids didn't know anything and didn't hear anything. When I stood quietly with them, it was as if I wasn't there. I learned that those families needed food, clothing and medicine for themselves and their children. They got those things free from Johnsons' store if they let Roy and Jimmy have their women.

They would do anything to survive. And they did.

White Man's Rules

In Putnam County, Georgia, where I grew up, white men had their own rules and blacks would do anything to raise their families. The blacks jumped to the white men's music and the whites played it loud and long.

Mom washed and ironed for Roy Johnson's family. One morning, she asked my brother Jabe and me to go to the Johnsons' house and pick up their laundry. I was about 18 then. When Jabe and I got to the back of Roy's house, we heard voices in the front.

I said, "Listen! That sounds like someone fighting. Let's go see."

My brother replied, "Are you crazy?!"

I said, "We won't get hurt."

My brother said, "No, we'll get killed!"

When we went around front, we didn't hear a sound. We looked, but didn't see anyone. There was a little hill with pine trees on it and we couldn't see through the trees. When I looked around, my brother had disappeared. I thought he'd probably gone home. Jabe wouldn't do the things I did. He was chicken. But he didn't get into trouble either.

Since I was at the front steps, I walked up to the front door. As I went to open it, I heard someone. I looked around and there stood Roy Johnson. He was angry. He said, "What do you think you're doing?" I couldn't speak. He surprised me and that scared me so bad that I couldn't find my voice. I was too busy looking at him to see if he was hurt from the fighting I had heard.

"Do you know where the back door is?" he asked. I nodded. Roy said, "Don't you ever come to my front door again!" I shook my head yes and went around to the back door to get the laundry.

On the way home, I was so mad at myself. Why did I go up them old steps? Why did I let Roy hurt my feelings? I always thought he was the kindest one in that family, that's why it hurt. I sure had been stupid. I was sure he thought I saw him fighting in the woods, but I didn't see anyone.

When I got home, my brother said, "Did you do anything?"

I nodded. I told him what had happened. I said the worst was that Roy hurt my feelings. It was his house, his rules. I shouldn't have gone to the front door of a white man's house.

I asked the Lord to forgive me.

Did you know that blacks couldn't go to the front door of a white man's house? How would you feel if someone told you you wasn't good enough to use their front door?

My brother Jabe right after he got out of the service in 1940.

Doing the Right Thing

Do you think doing the right thing is always easy?
Let me tell you about something that happened, that I'll never forget.

Daddy was the leader of the black men who worked on the Johnsons' farm. He didn't always speak up as much as he should have, but he didn't want to get anybody in trouble. My father and his friends were content with the way things were. They didn't know any better. Life had been that way ever since they had been in the world.

My brothers grew up fast. Work fell into their laps. They hired themselves out, working for Jimmy and Roy and others. My brother Jabe was smart. He knew what he wanted and he went after it.

One day, Jabe and my older brothers had a conflict with Daddy. They told him they weren't going to farm any more. They wanted to move somewhere else. Daddy couldn't work on the farm by himself. He had to agree with my brothers because he had no other choice. He told my brothers he would move if that's what they wanted. Then he told the neighbors he was moving. The neighbors were like Daddy. They were content with the way things were. But they talked among themselves and decided they would move too.

Jimmy and Roy never dreamed the men and their families would leave. They thought their workers would be there for the rest of their lives. They figured the men were too dumb to think for themselves. And they didn't think they knew where to go anyway. But within several months, all of the black families had moved off the farm. Roy and Jimmy hired other workers, but over the years those workers wouldn't take what Daddy and his men had taken, so they didn't stay long with the Johnsons.

Two or three years later, in 1942, some new workers Roy and Jimmy hired left just before the crop was to be gathered. Jimmy was sick and didn't get around good. Roy tried to get people to help with the crop, but nobody would come. They had gotten tired of being treated bad.

Daddy heard that Roy hadn't been able to find anyone to help bring in his crop. He felt bad about that. He went to see the men who had moved when he did. He asked them would they consider helping Roy and Jimmy. The men said no. There was a lot of talk about the night riders. They'd just hung three black men and set fire to some people's houses. After Jimmy got sick, Roy's and Jimmy's sons took over the job as night riders. Their parents had no say in what they did. Some say the boys got out of hand. Other counties hired them to take care of their counties too—in other words, to do their dirty work.

But Daddy was like a man who had a mission to fill. He asked the men again. They still said no. One man said he felt uncomfortable around Roy and Jimmy. They scared him. Another said they made him nervous. Daddy prayed and turned it over to the Lord.

One day, Daddy ran into one of the workers. He told the man how he felt. He said he just wanted to help Roy and Jimmy because they were in trouble. When the men used to work for them, Lord knows it wasn't all good, but it wasn't all bad either. The man felt sorry for Daddy. He told him to go ask the men again. So Daddy did and this time they said yes.

The next day, they headed for the farm. It got so hot the men got tired. One of them said, "This is a big mistake. It will soon be dark. The night riders could kill us and no one would ever find us. It's all James' fault. We should take him out somewhere and beat him ourselves!" They were talking about my dad! The man was mad. But the horse kept pulling the wagon toward the Johnsons' farm.

Jimmy and Roy lived near their store. When Daddy and the men arrived, all the white men were sitting out in front of the store. It was hot and the store had no fan. At first, they were glad to see the workers. But it wasn't long before they remembered that Daddy and his men had moved and left them, and they got mad all over again. They blamed Daddy for the men moving. They said Daddy took all their workers away with him. That wasn't true. The men went on their own.

The boys, Jimmy's and Roy's sons, said, "We never like niggers around 'less we're goin' to kill 'em." They were mad.

Daddy wondered if it was possible that the whites had changed or if he never really knew them. He was getting scared. He had never heard them say nothing like that. And he didn't want his men to get hurt.

Then Jimmy walked close to all of the men, black and white. He was sick and didn't know the workers had come to help them bring in the crop. He said, "Don't listen to nothin' them niggers has to say. They come to take everything we have. They'll kill us. I should've killed half of 'em before they moved."

Daddy thought to himself, have I made a big mistake? Did I misjudge the Johnsons? His friends wanted to go home. They were afraid the night riders would do something bad to them. Daddy was wondering how he could get his men out of there. But he believed God had sent him there for a reason.

Then Roy said, "Stop! I've been trying to get help for weeks. I can't get no one. I want them to stay."

Daddy was still trying to find a way out, but he had no answer. When he spoke, he said, "I heard you needed help, so I asked the men to come. We didn't come to fight or to call names. I thought we could help in some small way. I guess I was wrong." By then, it was dark. The men were scared to stay and scared to go home.

Roy said, "Give them some food. Tell them where to sleep."

Daddy knew the Lord had moved in a mysterious way, because Roy had stopped the young night riders from talking any more. He gave thanks to the Lord. But the men didn't sleep much that night. The whites had done everything Daddy had said they wouldn't do and the men thought the night riders would come after them. But nothing happened.

The next day, Daddy asked the men to forgive him for bringing them out there. He said he didn't know the whites were going to say all those things. The men told him, "Not today. We won't help." They were still mad at him. They all wished they were home. Daddy couldn't say what the white men would do next. He never heard them call anyone nigger before. Maybe he didn't know them after all.

All that week, Daddy and the men gathered the crop and put it in the barn. They were ready to go home. Roy, Jimmy and their families came out where the men were.

Roy said, "How much do we owe you for all this work?"

Daddy was thinking they'd never asked that before. They never asked you how much they owe you. They just give you whatever they want you to have.

He said, "For me, nothing. I don't know about the men."

Slowly, the men said, "Nothing." They were hurt and disappointed with themselves. They needed money, but didn't know how to ask for it. They'd been gone all week with nothing to show for it. But they didn't have enough courage to ask Roy for what they wanted and they didn't want Daddy to know how they felt.

Roy said, "Thank you all so much for coming and gathering my crop."

The boys said, "We're sorry about the bad things we said. We would never hurt you."

Jimmy wanted everyone to feel sorry for him, so he said, "I've been sick and haven't been myself. I didn't mean what I said."

Roy said to the men, "They just miss you because you moved away." Then he added, "We're going to sell the farm. Anything you see that you want, take it. We won't be needing it because we're moving to town."

The men talked between themselves. They didn't want the old junk. They just weren't satisfied because they wanted money. They needed to get paid. So did Daddy. But Daddy wanted to show the Johnsons that people can be good and decent and help one another, with no strings attached. He'd gone back because they were his friends and they needed help. He was gambling that Roy and Jimmy would pay them, but he wasn't going to ask them for a penny.

When their things were in the wagon, Roy told his boys, "Go get the boxes and put them in the wagon." He told Daddy and his friends, "Don't open them till you get home."

Going down the road, one of the men said, "Let's open those boxes. What's so important we have to wait till we get home? He didn't let us get nothing out of the store." Daddy said, "You'd have taken everything!"

Someone else said, "It may be an animal in the box and it's gonna hurt us."

Daddy said, "Lord, I hope not." He told the men, "When we get home, you can open the boxes."

When they got to Daddy's house and opened the boxes, they found so many good things inside, even things from the store. And there was an envelope with money in it and a note from Roy. It said, "This money is for your crop, and a little over. You won't have to borrow for the next crop. Thank you all for caring. Thank you for coming and not leaving when the boys and my brother was talking."

The men began to cry. They said, "James, we sorry. We was so scared. Thank you for taking us." Daddy was crying too. But he was crying because he was glad they were back home and didn't get hurt.

51

One man told him, "James, you look like a little old lady!" That made everyone laugh.

Daddy always believed they would get paid. He believed you should do people good. Don't do them bad because they did you bad. It's good to help someone in need. It makes you feel good. You will always get something back.

I imagine when two kinds of people as different as whites and blacks can find a way to live together with the Lord's help, it's something to be said.

I think my daddy was a really big man when he helped those white men, don't you? I'm proud to tell you about him.

This is my daddy, James Driskell, plowing the fields.
The mules' names are Ella and Haddie. (ca. 1940)

This is my family right after church, around 1938.
I am the third from the left. Our clothes were
made from flour sacks, fertilizer sacks, and meal sacks.

This is my brother Charlie and his wife Corinne.

Losing Dad and Mom

Daddy was sick a long time before we knew he was. He worked every day. He got so sick he couldn't get up and down. One day, he said he didn't feel good. That night, he died. He was in his late 40's. When we lost Daddy, it was like losing a brother and our best friend.

After Daddy passed, Mom couldn't get any help from the government for the children that were home. The youngest child was only seven. Daddy never worked any place but the farm. He never had a Social Security card and he didn't even have the right to vote.

Later, the children still at home decided they didn't want to work on the farm any more. They wanted to go to school in town and get jobs. So Mom moved to Milledgeville, and the children went to school. Some of the youngest ones later went on to college. Mom had her share of bringing up children and God was so good to her. She lived to see all her children grown up and out on their own—going in different directions, but still staying in touch.

One Saturday evening, Mom got so tired. The pain was too much. She just slept away. When Mom passed in April 1980, she was 79 years old. She had 45 grandchildren and 21 great-grandchildren. And she had got her right to vote.

After Mom died, we were like lost sheep. Some of us even stopped going to church. But when you're taught something, you may leave it for a while, but if it's good, you'll go back to it. Mom taught us well. We found our way back home.

My family's very important to me. Have you told your family lately how much you love them?

Going Back, Being Free

My brother Jabe and I talked about going back to where we'd lived as children. It had been a long time since we saw Roy and Jimmy Johnson. We didn't know whether they were living or dead. Jabe decided to find out where they were, so we could go see them.

I loved that farm where I grew up. Most of my sisters and brothers were born there. We had some good times, but there were sad times too. The Johnson brothers owned us. I don't think our parents even knew it. Whenever any of us talked about those times, I got angry. To get past those feelings, I thought Jabe and I needed to see Roy and Jimmy again. So we decided to go back for a visit. I needed to find the truth in a world I didn't understand.

Before we got to the Johnsons' store, my mind got carried away. We heard the white brothers were in bad health. But they still scared me. It was a hot day, but I was chilled to the bone. I kept thinking they could run us off with guns or hurt us in some way and there was nothing we could do about it. Although Daddy had passed away, I could hear him saying, "Stay out of trouble." If I had told Jabe how scared and nervous I was, he'd have run off and left me. I prayed and asked the Lord to protect us.

When we got to the store, Roy and Jimmy were glad to see us. But just being there made us uncomfortable. Roy looked old and tired, not all superior like he used to. Jimmy just looked like an old jim crow. He had always looked so evil. But they were both being nice. I was so nervous that I talked fast, asking about their family.

All at once Roy said, "You're your daddy's child. You never stop talking." I froze. But he laughed and walked over to where I was and said, "I miss your daddy. He was a good man. And a hard worker."

I thought to myself, when Daddy died you didn't send a card or any word. And why didn't you give receipts to Daddy and the other black men every time they bought something at your store? You went in and out of their houses, just like you lived there. You made the men feel like they weren't worthy of their families. You took their will and left them with nothing. I know what that can do to someone's mind. You kept them in their place and scared them to death with the night riders. But I looked at Roy and said nothing.

This is another picture of my brother, Jabe.

Then Jimmy asked if we had any pictures. We did. So Roy, Jimmy and Jabe began looking at them. They wanted to know all about our sisters and brothers. We didn't talk about long ago. I'm sure they were thinking about it, because I was.

I walked over to the window. It had been raining all morning and had just stopped. I thought about the time Daddy told Roy off and Roy walked away. But I also thought about the times Daddy had not stood up to Roy, especially about school. It wasn't all the white brothers' fault. Daddy could have told them, "My children are going to work part-time and go to school part-time." Maybe he had been scared. But how could he ever know what would happen if he didn't try?

When my brothers told Daddy they weren't going to work on the farm any more, that they were going to move to town, it hurt Daddy. To him, the farm was a way of life. He didn't know any other way. He was content with the way things were, because he never reached out and tried to do anything on his own.

I loved Daddy. He was a sweet man. But deep down he must have been afraid. He never tried to change the way things were. He taught us to never cross the white man's line. I don't think they would have done anything if we had. They acted the way they did just to scare us. But we will never know whether we would have gotten in trouble or not. Maybe we'd have gotten hurt. But we could get through it and start all over again. Daddy took that from us, and I think that was wrong.

I wished our parents had trusted us more. They were so busy protecting us they didn't even see us and what we wanted, or take time to try some of the things we suggested. As far as they were concerned, we didn't know what we were talking about.

While I was thinking about all this, the Johnsons' cook came out and brought us some cool water. She asked me did I want to go in the kitchen. I looked at Jabe and he looked miserable. I knew he wanted to leave, but I went with the cook. I thought about the time I had gone to the front door of Roy's house and tried to go up the steps, and how Roy had hollered at me and told me not to touch his door. And now here I was, going in his kitchen. I asked the cook did she want me to help her. She said to set the table. I wondered who was going to eat, but I didn't ask. When lunch got ready, she called the men in to lunch.

Jabe jumped up and said to me, "Let's go. I have some stops to make. I was just waiting for you to finish."

Roy said, "Oh, no. You're not leaving. We've thought about you so often. And now that you're here, you're going to stay and eat lunch." Jabe tried to wiggle out of it. He looked at me for help, but I did nothing.

Roy said, "Here, sit beside me." Jimmy said, "I'll sit on the other side." Then the cook came and sat down. They put all the food on the table. Jabe looked around and smiled. He had said we weren't going to stay and there we were—staying. Jabe was just like Daddy. Do whatever makes everybody happy. He never crossed the line with anybody.

We finished lunch, then left. When Jabe and I had arrived at the store, I didn't think anything had changed. But we'd had a nice visit. I began to see Roy and Jimmy in a different way. In God's eyes, we are all sisters and brothers. We are all just ordinary people. The struggle taught us how to survive.

I felt like I was shed of old clothes and had put on new ones. I felt free. *Can you tell how I felt about this?*

The Voice

December comes around slowly. With some people, it hits like a ton of bricks. The first day of December, people start to worry. How much money can they spend or do they have it to spend. They do this for a week. Then there's just two weeks before Christmas. They can't think or sleep.

That's how it was for me one year. Then I heard this little voice saying, "You should have started to put away a little money every month." I did, but too many things happened this year. Sickness. Some lost their jobs. Some couldn't find work. So many unexpected things. God knows we tried.

Then that little voice said, "No one told you it would be easy." But my heart was burdened down. I couldn't see my way out.

I heard the voice again, saying, "I promised never to leave you alone. All you have to do is ask." I stood there, the tears gone. I felt new and I walked different.

It got to be one week before Christmas. Things were still the same, but I saw them differently. So many people were worse off than me. So I got busy, praising the Lord and doing all the things that make my family happy for Christmas.

Sometimes I get so burdened down I think God forgot me. When that happens, I just remind myself that I am the one who forgot Him. And I listen for the voice.

My Husband, Mack

You want to hear about my husband?

I had lived with my parents until I was in my early 20's. My son David was born there in February, 1942 and I knew it was time for us to move on. Before Daddy died and when David was not quite a year old, we moved in with my uncle—Mom's baby brother—and his wife in Macon, Georgia. I had a job as a housekeeper. That same month, I met Mack at a rooming house run by one of his friends. He was renting one of Maggie's rooms.

Mack was raised in the country, but he had left Greensboro to live in Macon. His job was good, but boring. It was wartime and he was also a volunteer in the National Guard. He was clean-cut and nice. Today, my great-granddaughter would say he was "cool." Mack was a good man, but there wasn't anything exciting about him. He didn't even want to know how to be exciting. He seemed slow to me, which reminded me of my father—and I loved my father a lot. I always felt like I could take better care of my father than he did for himself. And I felt the same way about Mack. In fact, I think I fell in love with him because he was so much like my father.

I was the strong one, so I flirted with Mack to get his attention. When we went out together, he seemed to know everybody. It was nice to be with somebody like that. In November, we decided to get married by a justice of the peace. We didn't tell anyone until it was all over. But it didn't matter, because all of my family loved Mack. He was that kind of person.

Mack was a caring man. He loved kids, anybody's kids. He would play with them, just like my Daddy did. Mack loved David as if he were his own child. I had always wanted a little girl, but Mack and I never had any children of our own. Having as many kids as our parents had was something my sisters and brothers and I never talked about. I think it was because we were all so afraid it might happen to us.

Mack could take you anywhere and he looked like a million dollars. I don't think he ever bought any clothes for himself. He'd tell me,

This is my husband, Mack.

"I don't need that." It wasn't that he didn't like clothes. He just didn't want to spend any money for them. So I bought him everything—nice clothes and shoes. And when he got all dressed up, he acted like the president of the United States. *You see why I loved him?*

Mack was a homebody. He loved being home. He loved his dogs and loved playing with them. I could have anybody come to the house and he never said anything. Every weekend, he wanted to have a party. He was overweight and his doctor kept putting him on a diet. But when we had parties, we had lots of food and he could eat as much as he wanted without anyone noticing. We invited our families, friends and neighbors. Mack was president of the church choir, so they were at our house a lot. Having all those parties is how I got Mack to add a second bathroom, laundry, storage room, screened porch, and two more rooms to our home shortly before he retired.

Mack loved going to bed on time, usually around 9:30 p.m. That was just his bedtime. Our dogs went to bed with him. One dog would lie on the floor beside my bed and the other would lie on the floor beside Mack's. The house could be full of people, mostly his friends, but when 9:30 came around, he'd say, "You all stay as long as you want. I'm going to bed." Then he'd get the dogs in from the back yard and take them back to our bedroom. After a while, everybody got used to him. Shortly before 9:30, they'd begin to stand and get out of his way so he and the dogs could go to bed.

Mack didn't smoke or cuss, but I said anything I wanted to say. Sometimes he would look at me and say, "I thought you was a Christian!" I couldn't fight with him about anything. He'd pretend to snore and I'd think he was asleep, so I'd quit talking. He was fun to be around.

I loved being married to Mack.

My Father-in-law, General Lee

This story is about a very dear man. His name was General Lee Turner. He was my father-in-law, Mack's father. He lived on a farm in Greensboro, Georgia, with his wife Mamie and their children, Mack, Roy Lee, Frank, James, Pete, Jim, Luther, Charlie, Louella and Mary. Near the front of General Lee's house was the biggest oak tree I have ever seen. Its branches seemed to welcome everyone that came by. I first saw the tree in December 1943, when Mack took me to meet his family soon after we got married. The family's house was close to the big tree. There was a well by the house. It was lined with rocks and the water was cool.

My father-in-law could grow 'most anything he wanted to. He always grew more than he needed for his own family. He lived surrounded by neighbors. Some had large families and didn't have enough to eat. Some was sick, too old and couldn't work. It made no difference with General Lee. He shared food with anyone who needed it. His children used to say, "Our father would give away the house if anyone needed it." But the people shared with him too. If he needed help in any way, they were there.

General Lee was a good husband, father and friend. He loved going to church. Most of the families walked to church. On their way home, people would stop to talk or rest. Under the oak tree was a place to cool off and have a drink of water from the well. Sometimes the Lees made lemonade for them. I remember one summer General Lee barbecued hog and goat under the tree. He invited all the neighbors. He thanked them for sharing the tree with his family.

I loved that oak tree. If it could talk, I imagine it would say how happy it was to have everyone there.

This is my husband Mack's father
General John Lee Turner.

Having a Job and Saving Money

Mack and I wanted to better ourselves. We realized we had lived in the country most of our younger lives. So we moved to Atlanta in 1961 to look for work. We knew it wouldn't be easy. The city was so much bigger than Macon that I was terrified. Macon was more like country. My brother and his family lived there, but they were just getting by. With not much education, it was hard. But I could do many things. I could cook and sew, and read recipes and patterns. My sister-in-law, Ruby, knew a friend that used to work for people named Ralph and Beth Carroll. *(I'm changing the names of everyone in this part of my story to protect their privacy.)* That's how I got a job keeping house for the Carrolls.

I was so scared that first day I went to the Carrolls' house. But their home was beautiful, inside and out. Pretty flowers were everywhere. The Carrolls had two girls, Stephanie, seven, and Sarah, five. Mrs. Barton, Beth's mother, lived with them, but she was in and out all the time. Other people worked there too. Clyde was the yard man and Lilly came once a month to clean the silver. Lyla did the washing and ironing, and came whenever she wanted. She had been Ralph's nanny when he was little. She was like a beloved member of the family and they treated her that way.

When he hired me, Ralph told me, "No one stays long." He told me he thought the reason was Mrs. Barton. But he said, "I hire and I fire. Until then, you stay."

The first day, Mr. and Mrs. Carroll didn't tell me how they liked things and I was too scared to ask. That was a bad day for me. Dinner was awful. The meat was tough. The vegetables were overcooked. No one said how bad it was. I wanted them to tell me something. But they were afraid they would hurt my feelings and I was scared they would run me off, so no one said anything. On the way home, I decided not to go back, but I needed a job so bad. The next day things were better. The Carrolls talked to me.

I learned to get along with everyone. I loved the children from the first day and they loved me. I usually went to work at 10 a.m., stayed through dinner, then left around 7 p.m. When I got to work, the girls were gone to school. The Carrolls always left the newspaper out for me to read. Each morning, I had a cup of coffee and read the funny papers.

After I had worked there about two years, the Carrolls went on a vacation to Europe. One morning after they left, Mrs. Barton came in while I was drinking my coffee and reading the paper. She announced, "There's not going to be any paper reading this morning. You can drink your coffee while you work."

I was shocked! I was at a loss for words and I didn't know what to do. I laid the paper down, walked over to the sink and poured the coffee into it. Mrs. Barton said, "What are you doing?! Coffee and sugar cost money. Why did you pour it out?!"

I didn't answer. I could feel my eyes filling up with tears, but I told myself, "I am not going to cry!" I had already decided to quit, but I needed the job. Then I remembered what Ralph had told me. "I hire and I fire. Don't let Mrs. Barton run you off."

A little later, I went to talk with Mrs. Barton. I asked her where were the other people that worked there. She said, "With Beth and Ralph away, we don't need that much help, so they won't be back until Ralph gets home."

I asked her, "Do you pay them?" When she said no, I asked her who was going to do all the work.

She said, "You are."

I sat down and told her, "I am going to stay. I will do the work I was hired to do, but that's all. I would like for you to call the others back and pay them for this day. If you don't, I will call the Carrolls and tell them what you did." Then I went back to work. I didn't mind doing the other jobs. In fact, I could do everything. But it was the principle of the thing.

Mrs. Barton decided she would talk with me before Stephanie and Sarah got home from school. She had a good and a bad side, and she used them whenever it pleased her. She told me she would ask the others to come back and would pay them. She said everything would be the same if I promised I wouldn't call the Carrolls and tell them what she'd done. I told her that was fine with me. That was all I wanted. I didn't want to be a tattletale. I just wanted her to do the right thing.

As the years passed, Mrs. Barton and I came to respect and trust each other. She taught me how to buy clothes and other things, and when was the best time to buy them. I never knew these things because when I was growing up we made all our clothes at home. All I knew was if I needed something, I just bought it. But Mrs. Barton taught me how to look at labels, see what it's made from, if it needed special care and when the sales took place.

One day, Mrs. Barton told me, "You're going to the bank today."

I said, "What for?" She said I was going to save some of my money. I said, "No, I need it." My family had never grown up with money. We never had nothing to save. And I'd never been in a bank. But Mrs. Barton said I was going to save some money now, so we went to the bank. She showed me how to set up a savings account. I put $10 in savings that day and each month I'd put in whatever I thought I could afford, whatever was left over from my pay. It made me very proud.

Are you saving money in a bank? If you're not, you might want to start, because it's a good idea.

Learning How to Live without Mack

Do you know what it's like to lose someone you love?

This story begins in 1984. It is about losing Mack, learning how to live again, and getting to know my son and his family all over. Mack and I had been struggling so hard to survive all those years. When I was 62, I retired and worked for the Carrolls only on special occasions. Mack was going to retire in a few months. We were making plans to do some of the things we never had a chance to do. In a twinkling of an eye, all our dreams were gone.

One morning in October, Mack woke up sick. I rushed him to the hospital. A few days later, he was operated on for cancer. He got better, but never got well. On a Saturday night in May, he just slept away. As I stood by his bed looking down at him, I whispered to myself, "I am 65 years old. Mack and I been married almost 42 years. He gave us his love in his own special way. It's in our hearts to stay." I wept that night just for him. I felt alone and afraid. I had no desire to live.

My son David, his wife Georgia and their three children lived 1,300 miles away in Colorado. After Mack died, with the help of the Lord I lived alone for a year. David and Georgia come to see me almost every month. When my son gets tired of something, he lets you know. He finally told me, "This is too much. You sell your house and come live with us. I know you don't want to leave your sisters and brothers, but they have their own families."

I thought about it. David and his family had lived in Boulder, Colorado, for a long time. His children, Wanda, David Jr. and Patrick, came every summer to visit Mack and me. But we never got to see David and Georgia much. This was a chance to get to know them all over again. I prayed for strength and understanding. I wanted to always remember that my son and his wife offered to share their house for a while.

I was at a crossroad in my life, not knowing what direction to take. I felt sorry for myself. I was scared and I got mad. Why had God taken Mack from me? I felt ashamed for thinking that way. Then I heard a voice within say, "Be patient."

I said, Lord, what am I going to do? It's not easy living with old folks, especially when they're in their 60s. I didn't think I had long to live, so I decided to move in with David and his family. I thought it would be for just a little while, but it's been over ten years so far.

I will never forget the day I began to pack. I thought I was ready till I stood in the door and glanced around the house. With tears running down my face, I thought, "This is my treasure. It isn't worth much in money, but it's been my whole life all these years." I walked slowly from room to room, touching things and picking them up. It seemed like I never had seen them before. I had been so busy working and taking care of family that I had forgotten what I had. I thought how proud I was when I bought my things or when someone gave something to me. My children don't care about them. They call them junk. They don't want them. They'd sell everything in a garage sale, and if that don't work they'd call the Goodwill. I felt like I'd been stripped naked. My tears wouldn't stop.

After I moved to Boulder in 1986, there was times when I cried all night. I promised myself I wouldn't complain, no matter how hard the struggle was. I am sure I get on my family's nerves sometimes, but occasionally they get on mine. It's a hard job to know when to talk and when to stop. I prayed I'd do the right thing. I realized love is not enough. I had to have understanding and a whole lot of patience.

David isn't perfect, but he's a son I like telling people about. I hope when the time comes his sons will be as good as he is. He has a loving wife who goes a long ways and that's what Georgia is—a good wife and a loving person. I am blessed.

When I moved to Boulder, I knew only five people, all family. I was terrified, but I refused to stay home. I went to church. I did volunteer work. I worked in the yard—that's a good way to meet the neighbors. One of my neighbors, Marie, is so special. It's like I brought my best friend from home.

Nothing stays the same when we get old. My grandchildren have grown up and gone in different directions. Time moves on. Sometimes it leaves you standing alone. But I have found a new world. God has been good to me and I thank Him for it. *I hope you can tell what my life has meant to me.*

This is my family —
(in front) my son David, my great-granddaughter Chanté, and me;
(in back) my grandson Patrick, David's wife Georgia,
and my granddaugher Wanda.

Learning to Read

Do you know how to read? If you do, you don't know how fortunate you are. If you don't, get busy! It's never too late to learn.

I'd like to share with you my story about the Boulder Public Library's BoulderReads! (formerly called the Learning to Read Program). The program has done so many good and special things for me, it gave me a new life. I am 79 years old and I can read; I didn't learn till in my 70s, but it's never too late.

I always wanted to learn to read. I had no help. When I was young I was miserable; I wanted to read so bad because I wanted to leave home; I was scared to kind of leap out on my own. I wouldn't be able to find a job, find somewhere to live, and people can be so mean when you can't read. They ask you things, they know you don't know the answer; they just want to make fun of you. People can be cruel without even knowing it; I don't think they really know how bad it is, because they know how to read.

Once I got to Boulder I wanted to read worse than ever. I didn't know anybody, I didn't know where to go or what to do, and I was so scared that I would get lost and not find my way back. And everything was changed, nothing was familiar, and I didn't have Mack anymore to pay bills, handle things. I really wanted to be able to read.

When I read the Bible I didn't understand it and I wanted to understand what I read. And when you don't understand what you read, it's just like not reading at all because you don't know what the fine print says.

Mom and Daddy had just a little education. Their parents had no education, but what they taught at home was they thought education was important. We had a teacher part time but no money to pay her with. Families gave her things from the farm to pay for it. We didn't have no paper, we just wrote on what we could find which was usually paper bags. Not enough books to go around. The school was heated with wood but there was no wood, so we was cold all day. Sometimes the white boss said he would give us wood to heat the school if our families worked the fields, but when he was mad he didn't do it. The teacher was just out of high school herself. I didn't know about homework. The school was so far away, in bad weather we stayed home. I never had good clothes— just one good dress I would wash at night and dry by the fire. The older I got, the more I wanted to read. We were out of school so much, the boss looked for things to keep us out— in spring we helped with planting. When we wasn't missing school for working in the fields, I was missing school to help care for the babies because I was the oldest of 12 children. We washed the white family's clothes and washed their babies. We couldn't even walk up their unpaved driveway.

After I was grown up I had my own family. I had stopped wanting to read. It was still embarrassing. I did not want anyone to know I couldn't read so I was trying not to have many friends. Years passed and my husband, Mack, got sick. He was so sick. I was scared not knowing how to read. Mack took care of all the important things. I couldn't understand the small print he had always taken care of. I remember one night I got down on my knees so I could be close to the Lord. I said, "Don't leave me, and don't take Mack." I had tears so bad I couldn't see. I say to Mack, "What am I gonna do?"

He looked up and said, "You gonna be all right. You can do more than you think." He pass away that night. I was all alone. My son David lived so far away. David and his wife, Georgia asked me to live with them. I moved to Colorado. I didn't know anyone. David and Georgia went to work each day and their kids went to school. I was still alone. I dreamed about reading.

But the Lord look after me. I find my way back. I heard about the Boulder Public Library's BoulderReads! on TV. I never been so happy. The day of my appointment I was on my way, nothing could stop me. I remembered— Oh Lord, I didn't tell them I was old and in my late 60's and to top it all off I am black and from the South. Maybe I am too old and yet I want to read so bad. I don't know anyone but my family. I haven't seen many blacks. I never been north; I don't know how they do things. Do I have to go through the back door? What do I talk about? I wanted to run home. I decided, I'll just see what it is about. I met Diana Sherry, the program's director, and Virginia French Allen Shoemaker, who interviewed me. They were so nice. That's how I got in the program.

I am sure no one's been as low and lost as I have. I love telling people where I came from. I pray you get in the program. Don't get old like I did, you will miss so much. Not knowing how to read is bad. You miss so much, if you can't read. You miss the fun part. I got my self-esteem now. We all make mistakes, people can be so unfeeling. You may not tell people you can't read, but you only fool yourself. So be good to yourself and talk about it.

After I got in the program my first tutor was JoAnn and she didn't stay long because she went overseas with her husband. Next was Roger; I just had him a month because he just filled in while I was waiting for a new tutor. Then I had someone else and she didn't work out. Then I got Helen Schweitzer. Helen and I worked together for six years! She took me places— we visited the library in Central City and we visited the Boulder Carnegie Library for Local History. We read books about gold mining in Boulder County. I never read a book before the program, but now I have read 300 books! That's nearly all the books in BoulderReads! collection! I never knowed when I showed up for reading where Helen and I would go.

One day Helen had to leave to care for her father. She was gone six months, and while she was gone I got Ruth Rettich for my tutor. We worked together for about three years, even after Helen got back we worked together. For awhile I had them both! They was just like a captain and a lieutenant. They would find me books to read that I would like, and if one didn't find the right book, the other one would.

One day Helen told me I had to write. I hadn't been writing. I told her no, I couldn't spell and I couldn't write. She said yes, you will. I went home and said I'm not going back. When I got home I started thinking I was cutting off my nose to spite my face, if I wouldn't even try. So I called Helen and told her I would try and she said she knew I would. I was so put off with her because she already knew I would do it! I'd like to die when Helen moved to Nebraska to take care of her aunt. She volunteers at her library in Nebraska now.

Because of Helen I started writing and I love it so much. I just fell in love the first day of writing! I just started writing, not knowing what I was doing.

Ruth was just like a lost sister, we worked together for three years until she went to translate menus for the blind. But we are still friends today; twice a month we go to dinner and a movie. I worked with Helen until she had to move to Nebraska to care for her aunt. I about died when she left. But I still write to her and she writes to me. I hear

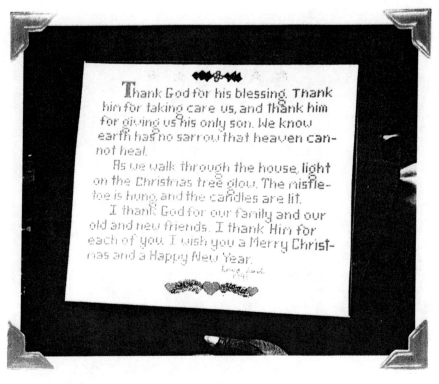

After I'd been in the BoulderReads! program a while, I wrote the first letter I'd ever written, and sent it to everybody I knew. My friend made a cross-stitch of that letter and this is a picture of it.

Here I am at the County Dinner Playhouse with Harlan and Mark, (Bill, Diana, and Emily not pictured) where we saw Agatha Christie's play, *Ten Little Indians*, which we read together beforehand.

from her all the time. Whenever we have something special at the Boulder Public Library I tell them both and send them special things (like the *Discoveries* book that has my story in it, published by BoulderReads!)

After Helen left I worked on writing a lot with my new tutor, Diane Quint. She helped me assemble my first stories. I worked with her for about a year until she moved to Iowa. Then I got matched to Loretta Goodenbour, but she was not a tutor as much as she was my secretary, my editor, my coach, and my mentor. And she still is. By then I was just writing all the time, and Loretta would help me by editing what I wrote.

When Diana Sherry asked me to get into a writing group with five men, I told her I couldn't do it because I was old and I knew they could write better than I could. But then Diana asked me again because she knew I liked to write and this time I said I would do it. I never been so full of excitement in my life. I had courage to try anything that the men tried, and I never worked so hard in my life. Diana would ask us to write about something, and we would do it. The men in the group weren't mean to me, if I needed to know something they would tell me, if I needed a ride they would give it to me. It was like I had five sons. I tried to do anything they did, and they stretched my mind— I had headaches some times! Harlan Davis was like a steady rock— I just admired him— he could write so well. I surprised myself in that class because I never dreamed I could do as good as that. Once our writing group read an Agatha Christie play together and then we went to see the play. There was a blizzard that night but we made it, and it was so much fun to see those words acted out by people.

Another time, Diana asked me to do a speech and I had never gotten up and spoken to people. For weeks I could hardly sleep, wondering what was gonna happen. Ruth was here and I spent the whole day over at Ruth's house with Ruth telling me, you can do it! And I was saying, I can't do it. That was the worst thing I had ever been up against and the best thing I had ever been up against. Because when it was all over (I cried all the way through the speech and there was a lot of people crying while they listened). That speech made me realize how far I had come, and it gave me the courage to talk about it. Before that I didn't have any self-esteem but it was wonderful after the speech.

Another one of the best times was when I saw my name in print and then even better, my story was put in a time capsule. *I'll tell you all about that in a minute.*

Once I was interviewed by the Boulder newspaper, the *Daily Camera*. That was exciting. All the neighbors wrote me a card about it and signed it, and they all saved me papers. It was like heaven on earth being interviewed by a reporter. I never dreamed I would talk to a reporter, much less be interviewed by one. Someone who saw the story wanted me to come and speak about my experience to a group of teenagers who were in a residential treatment center. The director, Michael Reynolds, asked me to come and talk to them, and Loretta went with me. Something strange happened to me on the way up there, we was just driving along and I saw the school and I still remember what it looked like— bare yard, no grass, and all the kids. It was so overwhelming, I could hardly take it. It was the best feeling. These kids sat there and didn't take their eyes off of me until I was through. I read them two stories about me, about having Parkinson's disease (so they would know why I was trembling because I shake when I am happy or sad), and I talked to them about not getting a chance to go to school. I told them they had to do things that need an education and about how hard it will be if they don't learn to read. I said don't be like me. It's your life. You got to live this life for yourself. Then I got letters and drawings back from all of them. They said they wanted me to come back, they really believed what I said and they knew I was telling the truth because I was talking about myself. Some of them said they were going to appreciate school a lot more now, and Michael told me later that they did— he really saw those kids change their attitude. They still invite me out sometimes.

Finally, Loretta started helping me assemble all my stories into a book. We called it, "Lady From the South", but now it has a new name. Diana and Loretta told me I should try to get it published. Today, you are holding my book!

I thank God for the Boulder Public Library's BoulderReads!, and I thank God that I can read. Learning to read is the best thing that ever happened to me.

Parkinson's

Have you ever been introduced to Parkinson's Disease? I was, about nine years ago, in 1991. I don't think you would like it. I wish I could describe all of the things it's capable of doing to your body. You can't win. There's no cure for Parkinson's. You won't get better. You only get worse.

So I decided to be friends with it. If I was a friend, it would lay off. But actually it got worse. So I decided to fight. I get so depressed sometimes I just want to run and never stop. I know that's no good, for I am responsible for my well-being.

When I begin to stiffen up, I tell it to stop. I say, "If you're going to hurt my legs, leave my hand alone. I wish you'd let me rest from pain for a little while."

I try to do everything the doctor says: I take my medication on time, eat right, go on long walks. Nothing seems to help. Parkinson's don't want to kill you. It just wants you to look bad. I tell it, "Leave my body alone. My body belongs to me. Take your trembling with you. Let my muscles go free." I have lost a little of my brain cells all the time. When it's gone, I won't have nothing.

The Parkinson's makes it so uncomfortable to dress. Buttons hurt my hand. It takes me a little longer all the time. I won't allow it to take and take. I am afraid to stop fighting. I may lose my will. I want to hold onto my mind long as I can.

I feel like I am in a glass box. People are passing and I call, but they can't hear me. I say to myself, "How did I get here?" I look up. My companion Parkinson's is sitting beside me.

Lord knows I don't want to complain, but I am so alone. I only complain to myself. I have to admit I like to fight sometimes. I decided to turn it over to the Lord and leave it there. God knows I been trying. I have fallen down several times. I didn't get hurt, but it's embarrassing.

I'll be writing one thing and my brain changes it to something else I have thought about. It changed my voice. I talk louder now.

Parkinson's will take your independence. It will try to stop you every way it can. I get so nervous sometimes. It will control your body if you let it. It will discourage you. That's why I have to keep on fighting.

Some days you need a shoulder to cry on so bad. I got in a support group. You feel free to talk and laugh sometimes. But I still miss someone close. I get so sad sometimes. I know I am not crazy yet, but I am headed in that direction.

I know one morning I will wake up and I won't remember my children and myself. It will be almost over. I walk over to the mirror and I won't recognize what I see. I will ask, "Where am I?" and try to touch my face. My arms and hand will be so stiff they won't move. My legs will tremble. I will hold something to keep from falling. I won't be standing straight, but bent over.

I say, "Lord, touch me with your powerful hand. The Parkinson's has taken everything from me. I am tired of fighting." I don't know what to do. I need someone to hold me tight so I can cry. I am afraid if I was alone I would never stop crying. At a time like this, I miss my mom so very much. I really need her.

Perfect Day with My Tutor

One of my happiest times growing up was walking to the field where Daddy worked, just to ride the mule back home. I loved to ride. There were some good times riding mules or driving wagons. Didn't even need a driver's license. Looking back, my poor Daddy needed the ride more than I did.

One day, I was talking to my tutor, Helen, about my days on the farm. Helen said her cousin Lee had horses and mules on his ranch. She said she'd ask him if I could come down and ride. When Helen told me it was all right for us to come, I thought about it and got scared. It had been so long since I rode a mule or been around one. I was thinking how would I get up on a mule. I had never been in a saddle. Growing up on the farm, I had always ridden bareback. And it hurt, too! But I didn't tell Helen how I felt. I thought I would just wait and see. After talking it over with myself, I calmed down and thought about the happy times I had long ago.

In December, Helen made arrangements for us to go down to Lee's ranch. It was a pretty drive from Boulder to Larkspur. Helen is a good driver and knew where she was going, so I just talked, looked and enjoyed the ride. We got down there about ten o'clock.

Lee is a jack-of-all-trades. He builds, fixes cars, and knows most everything about farming. He has everything to farm with. His place is beautiful. I could look up at the mountain from his ranch. He has a big white curly dog named Curly. The dog is sweet and friendly.

We went to the corral and met the other horses and mules. They all were beautiful. Lee got the mule out that he was going to ride. His name is Tuffy. I walked him around. He ate grass here and there. Lee got him ready to ride.

My mule's name was L.J. He was so pretty standing there in the sun. I loved him as soon as I saw him. He was all ready and waiting with his saddle on. I called him and he looked around. But he just couldn't make up his mind about me. After talking to L.J. for a while, he came around. I stroked him with my hand.

The big moment came. L.J. looked me over and thought if he wanted me to ride or not. I stood close to him. I said, "I know you are a free spirit. I love you. I hope you like me a little."

Then it was time to put up or shut up. I got up in the saddle with some help. I felt like I was high up in the air. Helen wasn't interested in riding. She took a walk instead. But Lee was ready and we were on our way. We went by a pig pen. The pigs started squealing. L.J. bucked, and onto the ground I went. I didn't have time to get scared or hurt. L.J. just looked at me as if he was wondering what I was doing down there. I got back on and off we went.

Lee has a riding trail. Some places the snow was deep. I realized L.J. had a mind of his own. When he decided he didn't want to go through the snow, he went around, without even asking. When we started home, I had to hold him back. It was a nice ride. Helen took pictures. L.J. was hot and wet. I rubbed him down. We put him back in the corral. He rolled around in the dust. L.J. is a special mule.

Helen, Lee and I walked around the ranch. It had been so much fun riding. We ate lunch at a pretty place in the country. I wished the visit would never end. We thanked Lee for a perfect day. And when we got back, Helen made me write all about it!

This is a picture of me on L.J., the mule,
at Helen's son's ranch.

This is a picture of me sitting next to the Boulder Public Library's time capsule, right after they sealed it with one of my stories inside.

Time Capsule

On Sunday, June 21, 1992, the new addition to the Boulder Public Library opened. That was the day for cutting the ribbon and putting in the time capsule. Diana, the program director, told me one of my stories was going to be in the capsule.

I asked, "Which one?"

She said, "The one about your grandmother, Big Mama."

I grinned to myself. I felt all warm inside. It was the first time anything big like that had happened to me. I whispered, "Thank you, Lord."

I stood there looking at the box. I had never seen another like it before. I said over and over to myself, "One of my stories is going into that box." I looked at my tutors, Helen and Ruth. I began to cry. I couldn't stop. I cried all the way home. The children thought something bad happened. Georgia asked, "Big Mama, what's wrong? Were you in a wreck?"

I am so happy to be in the reading program. It changed my life. At first, I didn't have the courage. I was terrified. But I promised to do my best. Now, when I read a book, I feel like I have been on a trip. I visit all kinds of beautiful places. I am thankful for everyone that touched my life since I been in the program. I am not where I would like to be, but I am not where I used to be.

When I think about my life before I found BoulderReads!, I shiver. I missed so much. Not knowing how to read is like being blind. I will tell anyone, "If you need the reading help, take that first step and walk on in. Do it for yourself. God will give you the inner strength you need. Learning to read will give you a new outlook on life. Next time, your story may make its way to the time capsule."

Thank you!

Well, you've been good to walk with me and listen to my whole story. It's been good to tell you. When you think about it, I've had a good life. The way things are going, I won't never go through the back door again.

JANET DRISKELL TURNER was born in 1920 and grew up in rural Georgia. Her memoirs tell of deep poverty tempered by ingenuity, oppression by the white landlord tempered by forgiveness, harshness of life tempered by community support and religious convictions. It is a story of illiteracy cured by literacy, and of a courageous woman who learns to read as a great-grandmother. Pull up a chair and listen to Janet as she shares her stories.

0-595-32450-9